DRUGS AND YOUR FRIENDS

Friends must make choices about following the examples of their peers.

THE DRUG ABUSE PREVENTION LIBRARY

DRUGS AND YOUR FRIENDS

Sue Hurwitz and Nancy Shniderman

THE ROSEN PUBLISHING GROUP, INC.
NEW YORK

To Gene
S.H.
To Jeff
N.S.

And a Special Thank You to:
James J. Khalili, Ph.D
Psychological Development Services
Olathe, Kansas
and
The Kansas Department of Social and Rehabilitation Services:
Alcohol and Drug Abuse Services
Topeka, Kansas

Published in 1992 by The Rosen Publishing Group, Inc.
29 East 21st Street, New York, NY 10010

First Edition

Printed in Canada

The people pictured in this book are only models; they, in no way, practice or endorse the activities illustrated. Captions serve only to explain the subjects of photographs and do not in any way imply a connection between the real-life models and the staged situations shown.

Library of Congress Cataloging-in-Publication Data

Hurwitz, Sue
      Drugs and your friends/by Sue Hurwitz and Nancy
      Shniderman. — 1st ed.
      (The Drug Abuse Prevention Library)
      Includes bibliographical references and index.
      Summary: Discusses peer pressure and drug use and the
      importance of making the right choice.
            ISBN 0-8239-1263-9
            1. Teenagers—United States—Drug use—Juvenile
            literature. 2. Teenagers—United States—Alcohol
            use—Juvenile literature. 3. Children—United
            States—Drug use,Juvenile literature. 4. Child–
            ren—United States—Alcohol use—Juvenile
            literature. [1. Drug use. 2. Substance abuse.]
            I. Shniderman, Nancy, 1956–. II. Title.
            III. Series
            HV5824. Y68H87 1991
            362.29'083—dc20   90-9113
                                                                      CIP
                                                                      AC

Contents

*L*ife is full of choices. Some choices are good and good for you. Some choices are bad and not good for you. You have a *right* to make choices that are good for you. You are in control of making choices that affect your life.

Today you face more choices than ever. And it is not always easy to make a good choice. You need to think about what will happen after you choose. You need to have good information to make a good choice.

Sometimes you do not have time to think about what will happen. Sometimes you are rushed to make a choice without good information. Sometimes you are pressured by your friends to make a bad choice.

This book is about drugs and your friends. Both drugs and friends involve making choices. This book explains some drugs that are common. It discusses what those drugs can do to your body and mind. It tells you what might happen if you make a bad choice. It lists places you can go for help.

This book also looks at how friends can help you make good or bad choices. It discusses ways you can say "No" to friends who try to control your choices.

You must make your own choices if you want to be in control of your life. That is your *right*. The information in this book can help you make good choices.

But the choices are up to you.

And what happens because of your choices is also up to you.

Liquor is legal for adults and easy to get—but is an illegal drug for teenagers.

Drugs—What They Are and What They Do

You see drugs used on TV shows and in movies. You see ads for alcohol or tobacco in magazines and newspapers. You may see people smoke, drink, or use drugs. You may see someone sell drugs. You may know someone who does it.

Using alcohol, tobacco, and drugs looks like fun. It looks grown-up. It looks like something to do. You may be curious.

But do you really know about drugs and what they do? Will someone who sells drugs or alcohol or tobacco really tell you that they are harmful?

A drug is a chemical that causes changes in the way you feel and think and behave. Some drugs are healthful. Those

9

10 | drugs are called medicines. It is not against the law to buy them or to use them. It is also not illegal for pharmacists to sell them.

This chapter is about some drugs that are harmful and illegal. It also describes some drugs that are not illegal but are harmful.

Alcohol

Alcohol is the number one drug problem for young people in America today. In 1985, about 4.5 million young people between the ages of 14 and 17 were involved in alcohol-related problems. Many were arrested. Many were involved in accidents including drowning and fires.

Alcohol kills about 98,000 people each year. More than half of them die in auto accidents.

Alcohol is easy to get. Alcohol is not illegal to buy or to use for people over a certain age. But alcohol is *always* harmful. The younger you are, the more harmful it is to drink.

About 10 million people in the United States depend on alcohol. These people are called *alcoholics*. They find it hard or impossible to do without alcohol. They are *hooked*. Alcohol can easily become habit-forming. Some teenagers become alcoholics less than six months after taking their first drink.

Alcohol is a chemical formed by fermenting the sugar in grains or fruits. The kind of alcohol found in beer and wine is called ethyl alcohol. Ethyl alcohol is also found in hard liquors such as whiskey, gin, vodka, and brandy.

Alcohol is a mind-changing drug just like cocaine or crack. It takes only about fifteen minutes for alcohol to travel through your bloodstream to your brain. Alcohol depresses or slows down your *central nervous system.* The central nervous system controls the way you stand, walk, and speak. Alcohol also slows down muscle movement.

At first a drinker may feel relaxed. A drinker may get a feeling of pleasure called a "high." But then the drinker begins to lose self-control. He or she may not think clearly enough to make good choices. He or she may take unnecessary risks or say or do things he or she is sorry for later. The drinker may talk loudly and become abusive. The drinker may become clumsy.

Long-term drinking can damage your brain. It can also damage your liver,

12 kidneys, heart, and stomach. Alcohol can cause skin problems and diarrhea.

But you don't need to be an alcoholic to have serious problems from drinking. Even one drink can give you a pounding headache, or *hangover.* One drink can make you vomit—or wish you could! One drink can cause you to fall and hurt yourself. One drink can make you reckless and get you into trouble with others or the law. Even one drink can cause you to have an auto accident and maybe kill yourself or others.

Even one drink is too many.

Even one drink is illegal.

Tobacco

About one million teenagers and children in the United States start smoking every year. Every state has laws saying a person must be over a certain age to buy and to use cigarettes. Almost everyone knows that tobacco and tobacco smoke are harmful to your health.

But many people still make poor choices. Many people still smoke cigarettes, cigars, or pipes. Some teenagers also use *snuff* in their nose or chew tobacco even though tobacco is harmful and illegal.

A teenager who starts smoking cigarettes is making a very poor choice.

14   Nicotine is a colorless, oily chemical in tobacco. Nicotine is habit-forming and makes it hard to stop smoking once you start. Smokers quickly become used to having nicotine in their body and they crave it. Nicotine is a poison that is used as a weed killer. Large doses of nicotine can kill you.

Nicotine travels from your lungs into your bloodstream in seconds. It speeds up your heart and nervous system. Nicotine also slows down the amount of blood that reaches your heart. And that is harmful.

Smokers say that smoking helps them relax. But they also complain of sore throats, coughing, shortness of breath, and dulled sense of taste.

Carbon monoxide is a gas in the fumes that come out of a car's exhaust pipe. Carbon monoxide is also in cigarette smoke. It is dangerous to the smoker. It is also dangerous to nonsmokers who are near someone smoking.

Tar is a cancer-causing chemical in tobacco. Tar is the brownish, sticky stuff that smokers get on their fingers and ashtrays. Tar is made of several hundred different chemicals. It can damage a smoker's lungs when it is inhaled with cigarette smoke.

Smoking cigarettes greatly increases the   *15*
risk of many kinds of cancer. Lung cancer
is ten times more frequent in smokers
than in nonsmokers. But a year after a
smoker stops smoking, the risk of lung
cancer is greatly reduced.

Smoking tobacco also increases the risk
of cancer of the mouth, throat, voice box,
and esophagus (the tube from your mouth
to your stomach). Both bladder and kid-
ney cancer are related to tobacco smoking.

Smoking in America dates back to before Christopher Columbus arrived here in
1492. American natives showed Columbus
how to roll tobacco leaves and smoke
them. Columbus took the habit back to
Europe.

In those days, people didn't know how
harmful it was to smoke. But now we do.
Now nonsmokers don't want to breathe
the carbon monoxide from smokers' cigarettes. More and more public places limit
where smokers may smoke. Warnings are
printed on the packages of cigarettes. It is
no longer "cool" to smoke. Smokers are
less and less welcome.

Today everyone knows that cigarette
smoke is dangerous. Many places will not
hire people who smoke, or will allow them
to smoke only in certain areas. A smoker

16 is becoming more and more limited in his or her choices.

The best choice a smoker can make is to stop smoking!

Marijuana

Marijuana is also called "grass" or "pot." Marijuana is made from a plant called *Cannabis sativa.* It contains more than 400 chemicals. THC, tetrahydrocannabinol, is the main chemical in marijuana. The more THC in a cigarette or *joint,* the greater the high. There is more THC in today's marijuana than in past years. So there is greater harm in smoking it either in a cigarette or a pipe.

At first a smoker may feel relaxed and silly. But after a while the user becomes sleepy.

Marijuana increases your pulse rate and makes your eyes bloodshot. Your mouth becomes dry. Marijuana affects your brain, making it hard to concentrate. Marijuana also affects your sense of timing and muscle movement, making it dangerous to drive after smoking.

Some users have panic attacks and fear "losing control." Long-term use of marijuana also makes a user lose interest in

Trying a joint may seem harmless, but it can damage your body and your mind.

18 life. That leads to learning problems at
school and makes it hard to keep a job.

Marijuana smoke contains even more
cancer-causing chemicals than tobacco
smoke and is dangerous to a smoker's
lungs. And smoking tobacco and marijuana together is even more harmful.

Marijuana is stored in the fatty parts of
body cells. Since one third of your brain
has these fatty cells, it takes a long time
for marijuana to leave the body. The
chemicals from a single joint can take a
month to leave a smoker's body even
though the smoker felt the high for only a
few hours.

Drug abuse often starts with alcohol,
tobacco, or marijuana use. These three
drugs are called "gateway" drugs because
they often lead to use of other drugs.
When young people use these drugs to
avoid facing the problems of growing up
they are more likely to try other drugs too.

Cocaine and Crack

Cocaine is a drug made from leaves of the
coca plant, which grows in South America.
Cocaine is usually made into a fine white
crystal-like powder. When the powder is

You can say "no" to friends who offer you crack or other drugs.

Drug-addicted teens may steal from friends to buy their next fix.

sniffed or *snorted* into the nose it is absorbed into the user's blood Cocaine can also be injected, or shot into a user's vein.

Crack is a form of cocaine that is made into large white crystals. Crack is smoked, or *freebased.* When crack is absorbed into a user's lungs, the effects are usually felt within a few seconds.

The crack high is more powerful than the cocaine high. The crack high lasts five or ten minutes. It is followed by a powerful *crash,* or withdrawal symptoms. This leaves the user tired, depressed, and irritable. That is what makes crack so habit-forming. The user wants more crack right away to avoid these bad feelings.

Users become dependent on crack from the first time or two they use it. After trying crack only once, a person may be hooked.

Cocaine and crack affect the body in the same way, but the effects of crack are faster. The user's heartbeat speeds up greatly. Blood vessels tighten, and that raises the user's blood pressure. Pupils of the eyes dilate. Less oxygen reaches the brain. This can result in mental problems and in stroke. Cocaine users also run the risk of having fluids settle in their lungs.

An evening of drinking, doing drugs, and driving can lead to a terrible injury or even death.

If the cocaine, or "coke," is snorted, the chemical damages the lining of the user's nose.

Cocaine is also harmful to the reproductive systems of men and women. During pregnancy cocaine use can cut off oxygen to the unborn child. The child may be born addicted to cocaine and die.

We all have heard of famous people who died from using cocaine and crack. These deaths are not usually from an overdose but because coke and crack are absorbed so quickly by the body. The increased heartbeat causes a heart attack.

No one can tell how his or her body may react to a drug. Some people may get by for a long time without a bad reaction. But some people die from trying crack only once.

Heroin

Heroin is a drug made from opium, which comes from a poppy plant grown in the warm climates of Asia. Heroin is made into a white powder that may be inhaled or injected.

When heroin is injected into a vein, the user risks damaged veins and sores and needle marks on his or her arms. If a user shares a needle or uses a dirty needle there is the added risk of infection or catching *AIDS.*

Heroin gives the user a powerful high followed by a feeling of relaxation. But it soon takes more and more of the drug to reach the high. The heroin is taken not for the pleasure of the high but to avoid the bad feelings of the crash.

Someone using heroin has a slower heart rate and shallow breathing. A user may become restless, drowsy, or feel like vomiting. During the crash the user may have painful cramps, diarrhea, chills, or sweating for a week or more.

The effects of heroin last three to six hours. During this time the user keeps wanting more and more heroin. There is a big danger of overdosing during this period.

Is using drugs really worth the risk?

Do you really think a mature person would harm his or her body and mind that way?

That is something you need to think about when you make your choice about drugs.

That is something you need to remember when your friends try to make your drug choices for you.

A drinking habit can lead to a lonely life as the addict loses friends and relationships.

CHAPTER 2

Friends and Peer Pressure

Max's Friends Use Alcohol

Max and Josh had been friends since elementary school. But after they started middle school last year Josh began hanging out with older kids. He no longer had time for Max.

Josh nodded when he passed Max in the halls at school. But he spoke to Max only once all year—when he asked to copy Max's math homework. Max offered to help Josh with his math. But Josh just stormed away in a huff.

So Max was surprised when Josh called one Saturday.

"Want to come over?" Josh asked. "My parents are going out and we'll have the TV all to ourselves!"

28

Max wasn't sure whether he should trust Josh, but he finally agreed.

"Want a beer?" Josh asked after Max had walked over and they started watching a horror movie on TV.

"No," Max told him. "I'd rather have a soda." He looked hard at Josh. "You know I don't drink!"

Josh handed Max a can of soda, then popped the top of his beer. "Maybe you should try alcohol. Drinking breaks up the boredom."

"I'm never bored enough to mess up my mind," Max said.

A while later two of Josh's new friends dropped in.

"Do you have a beer?" Roger asked as he and Bill swept through the door.

"No problem!" Josh hurried off to the kitchen. He returned with four beers and offered Max one.

"No, thanks," Max told him, picking up his soda. "I'm fine."

"What's wrong? Are you too chicken to drink?" Roger asked, staggering over to a chair. He pushed the extra can of beer toward Max. "Do yourself a favor. Grow up a little!"

Max ignored Roger and pretended to be interested in the movie. He watched Josh

Peers can pressure you to do drugs or drink—but a good friend
can give advice and comfort you when you're feeling down.

30 from the corner of his eye. Josh was chug-
ging down his beer as if there were no
tomorrow. Max felt sorry for him. If
drinking was the only way to be one of
these guys he was glad he was left out!

"Here, drink this!" Roger insisted in a
slurred voice. He pulled a bottle of whiskey from his jacket pocket and grabbed
Max's soda. He tried to pour whiskey
through the opening of the can, but he got
more on the floor than in the soda. "Try it,
don't be such a baby!"

"I can't spare the brain cells!" Max
joked. He set the soda firmly on the table.

Roger and Bill were gulping their third
beers just as Josh threw up. All over the
rug! Roger and Bill both laughed as if
Josh done had done something great in-
stead of something gross.

Now Max knew why he hadn't heard
from Josh. Josh was too busy drinking!
Max knew why Josh didn't do his homework. He was too sick and too cranky
from drinking! But that was Josh's problem, not his.

Max decided to help Josh get safely to
bed, then get away from the craziness.
"Do you want some help before I leave?"
Max asked Josh. "I'm going home."

"Thanks, Max," Josh said weakly. "I can manage, I'm used to this."

"That's your choice," Max said, reaching for his jacket.

Max made his choice. He was out the door!

Roger and Bill didn't seem to notice. And Josh was too drunk to care.

As Max walked home, he thought about Josh. He knew that Josh's father was a heavy drinker, but he hadn't realized that Josh also used booze.

Max planned to talk with Josh about joining a support group when he was sober enough to listen. Max had heard that meetings of Alcoholics Anonymous—AA— were usually a big help to recovering alcoholics. He would also tell Josh about Alateen, the support group especially for teenagers.

Max made several good choices to avoid letting his peers involve him with alcohol. He said "No" when Josh offered the first beer. He also gave Josh a look that said he meant it. Then he told Josh he didn't want to mess up his mind. That showed Josh that Max knew the results of using alcohol.

Max tried two methods of avoiding peer pressure when Roger spiked his soda.

Cigarettes can be so habit-forming that addicts may have to
sneak a smoke between other activities.

First, he ignored Roger. Second, he tried to joke off the pressure.

Finally, Max realized that he couldn't help his friend until Josh was ready to help himself. So, wisely, Max left the scene to avoid any further problems.

Still, Max hoped to use positive peer pressure on Josh to get help for his alcohol problem. Since Josh let Roger and Bill make bad choices for him, maybe he would let Max suggest some good choices. With the help of AA, Josh probably could get his alcohol problem under control.

Max only hoped it wasn't too late.

Darcy's Friends Use Tobacco and Marijuana

When Rose called Darcy and asked her to go to Megan's slumber party, Darcy said "No."

"It will be fun, Darcy," Rose coaxed. Don't you want to see all our friends?" "I've been to Megan's parties before," Darcy said. "Kathy and Charla will probably chain-smoke all night!"

Darcy swallowed the lump in her throat as she suddenly remembered her grandmother. Grams was a heavy smoker and live the last ten years of her life battling

34 emphysema. Darcy remembered how Grams' lips turned blue from lack of oxygen. She remembered how Grams struggled for every breath. Darcy also remembered how Grams finally was dependent on an oxygen machine just to live a few years longer.

Darcy was not going to let that happen to her!

Grams' doctor had told her that addiction to nicotine was harder to beat than addiction to most other drugs. The doctor was right. Grams tried many, many times to stop smoking. But she couldn't stop even though her life depended on it.

"I know you don't approve of using tobacco," Rose said. "I don't either. But just because others use tobacco doesn't mean we have to join them!"

"I don't even want to be exposed to secondhand smoke from someone else using tobacco!" Darcy insisted. "That carbon monoxide is just as harmful as if you use tobacco yourself."

Rose sighed. "Oh, Darcy, be a sport. You and Megan are the only ones who are old enough to drive. Why don't you take me over to Megan's and see how things are going? If Charla and Kathy smoke as much as last time, you can leave. I'll call

Trying to kick a smoking habit is hard, but it's one of the best choices you can make.

36 | my parents in the morning to come after me."

"Okay. But don't try to pressure me into staying if I decide not to, Rose. You know I make my own decisions."

"Agreed!"

Darcy and Rose were the first to arrive at Megan's house. They listened to music in Megan's room while they waited for Kathy and Charla. They talked about what they had been doing since school ended the month before.

Darcy was enjoying herself. She hoped Charla and Kathy weren't still so dependent on tobacco that they would ruin the evening.

But Darcy soon found out.

When Charla and Kathy strolled in, Charla was puffing on a cigarette. They sat down on the floor, and Kathy opened her purse. "We're really going to have a party tonight!" Kathy boasted. "I took some of my sister's pot!"

"I haven't had a joint in nearly a month!" Charla exclaimed. She blew three smoke rings into the air, then crushed out her cigarette. "I can't wait to get high!"

"I thought we were going to play cards or something," Rose reminded her friends.

"Are you two just going to sit around and smoke all night again?"

"Don't be a nag, Rose," Kathy complained with a sigh. "Grow up! Try this weed and relax a little." Kathy lit the marijuana and inhaled deeply. She closed her eyes and leaned back against the side of Megan's bed, handing the reefer to Rose.

"I'm not in the mood." Rose made an excuse and didn't reach for the marijuana cigarette.

But Megan did. She inhaled slightly, then began coughing. She immediately handed the grass to Charla.

Darcy was uncomfortable. She had planned to leave if her friends started using tobacco. Now that they were experimenting with marijuana, she was definitely leaving.

"I'm going," Darcy told Rose. "Do you want to come along and we'll stop for pizza?"

"You don't know what you're missing!" Kathy said as Darcy took the car keys from her purse.

"Oh, but I do!" Darcy responded. "I'm missing several kinds of cancer, heart disease, and emphysema!" Darcy turned to Rose. "What did you decide, Rose?"

38 "Pizza sounds good," Charla interrupted before Rose could reply. "Why don't we all go for pizza?"

"I'm sorry you don't want to stay, Darcy," Megan said sincerely. "But I understand. Maybe some other time?"

"Yeah," Darcy promised.

"Me, too," Rose echoed. "Maybe another time."

"Pizza does sound good," Megan decided. "Since you aren't coming back here, I'll drive and we'll meet you there."

"No, Megan. It's dangerous to use marijuana and drive. Your reactions are slower now, and your risk of an accident is higher. Your thinking won't be normal for up to twelve hours. You all ride with us and I'll bring you back."

"Thanks, Darcy. We'd love to!" Kathy chimed in. "Let's go before Megan's parents find out that we've been smoking pot!"

"Yeah, let's!" Charla agreed between giggles.

"I don't know why I let Kathy tempt me into trying marijuana," Megan admitted later as they ate. "I know there are more cancer-causing chemicals in one joint than in a whole pack of cigarettes. I guess I was just curious."

Even if friends want you to drink, it's still your decision.

40 "You should never use two drugs at the same time!" Rose told Charla. "Mixing chemicals from tobacco and marijuana can be deadly!"

Charla didn't answer Rose. The marijuana high had worn off, but she couldn't concentrate on what Rose was saying.

"I'm going to try to cut down on smoking," Megan blurted out. "My cousin Gwen took a no-smoking class given at one of the hospitals. She stopped smoking in six weeks. I'll have a serious talk with Gwen and find out what else helped her quit."

"That sounds like a good choice," Darcy told Megan. "You might also check out no-smoking videos from the library."

Megan sighed. "Thanks for suggesting the pizza and getting us out of the house, Darcy. When you drop us at home, I'll insist that Kathy doesn't take any more marijuana out of her purse."

Later, as Darcy drove her friends back to Megan's house, she thought about the evening. The marijuana had made Kathy paranoid—she was afraid her sister would miss the joints or that Megan's parents would discover her drug use. Charla became silly and couldn't stop giggling. Megan felt guilty and probably would not experiment with drugs again. Rose felt relieved to get away from the peer pressure to use pot.

How did she feel? Darcy was sorry she had wasted the evening. She should have gone to a movie with Rose as they usually did on a Saturday night.

Darcy had a strong reason to avoid using tobacco. She had watched her grandmother die a slow death. She had vowed not to abuse her mind or body with drugs or tobacco. Because Darcy knew what was best for her, she wasn't influenced by her peers.

Darcy set limits before going to the party. She told Rose that she would leave if their friends used tobacco. When the situation occurred, Darcy knew exactly what to do. She didn't even need to think about making a choice.

Rose, Darcy's best friend, was also drug-free. But Rose was anxious to appear grown-up since she was one of the younger members of the group. Rose wasn't as assertive as Darcy when it came to resisting peer pressure. But she was learning.

Darcy suggested a different activity—to go for pizza—to help Rose get away from

Drug and alcohol abuse can make you violently ill.

peer pressure. Darcy showed Kathy that she knew the effects of smoking both tobacco and marijuana. Darcy made it clear that she chose not to use them.

When Darcy saw that Megan planned to drive, she offered to take everyone else along to keep Megan from driving after using drugs.

Finally, Darcy encouraged Megan to get advice from someone who had kicked the tobacco habit. She remembered that nicotine was so addictive that her grandmother never could stop smoking.

But Darcy hoped that Megan would!

Brad's Friends Use Cocaine and Crack

Brad's vision was still blurred. His muscles still twitched. He was so jittery that he could barely stay on the chair in the counselor's office. He felt like running out of the school. But that would only get him in deeper trouble.

"You know schools don't need search warrants to search students' lockers," Mr. Johnson explained.

Brad finally focused his attention on the counselor. He and Tony had just snorted all the cocaine they had bought earlier from a guy behind the school. He

44 wasn't worried that anything would be found in his locker.

"I know," Brad answered as he stared across the desk at Mr. Johnson.

"Are you aware that the federal Anti-Drug Abuse Act of 1986 made punishments for possessing or selling drugs much tougher?"

"Yes."

"Pushers and users aren't getting off with suspended sentences anymore. In the next few years punishments for offenders will get even tougher."

Brad didn't answer. He felt like puking. His coke was wearing off and he wondered if he would die. He almost wished he would. The crashes were so painful that he felt miserable just knowing what was ahead for him.

At least he hadn't smoked crack as Tony and his friends had wanted him to the night before. He had watched Tony's crack crash and it was unbearable!

"Urinalysis, the testing of urine to see if a person has used drugs, is a growing practice," Mr. Johnson continued. "Urinalysis is used not only by law enforcement officers but also by employers, schools, and colleges now."

"Umm." Brad knew about urinalysis. There was no way to beat it. If you used drugs and were tested, the book was thrown at you. Everyone had heard about athletes who lost jobs, titles, and medals because they tested positive to a urinalysis.

"If drugs are found in your locker, you'll be suspended from school." Mr. Johnson cleared his throat. "A suspension from high school for drug use could limit your opportunities later for college or a job."

Brad didn't care. Tony had suffered a bad reaction to the coke. After Brad had gone to the office for help, Tony was taken to the hospital. Unconscious. Maybe dead. What did it matter if he was thrown out of school? He couldn't say he deserved better.

Mr. Johnson answered the buzz from his intercom. Nothing illegal had been found in Brad's locker. He was free to go.

But how free was Brad? Would his close call with the law make him stop using drugs? Would he remain a slave to coke?

"Come in and see me if you ever feel like talking," Mr. Johnson told Brad. "Talking to someone about your problems usually helps."

Brad sighed. "I'd like that, Mr. Johnson. I'll come in tomorrow. Right now I'm going to the hospital to see Tony."

The United States has the highest rate of teenage drug use in the industrialized world. Brad and Tony were part of that number.

When Tony was pressured to smoke crack the night before, Brad knew he was getting dragged deeper and deeper into a life-style that he didn't want. He claimed that his parents expected him home immediately. Then he left.

But Brad was wondering how to break the drug cycle. Now Mr. Johnson had given him an option.

Brad was ready to get help by talking to Mr. Johnson. He realized that drugs would ruin his future if he didn't stop now. He only hoped that Tony would be able to join him the next day.

Lee's Friends Use Heroin

Lee came from a nice family. She never needed to worry about money or clothes. But she didn't feel accepted by her peers at school. She was fourteen and had no friends—either male or female. And that made her very unhappy.

Making friends who are drug-free will help you stay that way too.

48

Paula, a girl in Lee's history class, asked if Lee wanted to go to a party with her cousin, Dale.

Lee was thrilled and agreed.

When Dale came to pick Lee up for the party, she noticed that he was very thin and coughed a lot. But he was friendly, and Lee enjoyed the attention.

At the party, Lee saw many people lying around looking sleepy. She was disappointed that the party wasn't more lively with people dancing and talking.

Soon, Dale asked Lee if she used heroin.

"Aren't you worried about AIDS?" Lee asked.

"I'm not stupid enough to *mainline*. I don't shoot up my veins," Dale boasted. "I roll junk inside a cigarette and smoke it!"

Dale "fixed" a cigarette with heroin and took a drag off it. Then he handed it to Lee. "Take a puff, Lee, " Dale coaxed. "It's fantastic!"

Lee was eager to be accepted into the group. She didn't think much about what might happen if she became dependent on heroin. So Lee began using heroin to please Dale. But she didn't find heroin fantastic at all.

Before long Lee was addicted to heroin. **49**
She was doing things she had never
thought she'd do. She was lying to her
parents. She was cutting classes to see
Dale and get more heroin. The heroin left
her too sleepy to do her homework. She
often slept in class, too. Her grades
dropped, and she was barely passing her
classes.

When Lee was awake, she spent most of
her time looking for more heroin. She
began selling her clothes and jewelry to get
money to help Dale buy junk, or smack.

Finally Lee's parents realized something
was wrong. They insisted that Lee stop
seeing Dale and her new friends. They
also demanded that she get treatment for
her addiction.

Lee knew she faced some difficult
choices. She could fight her parents' advice and continue to see Dale and to use
heroin. After all, she was almost fifteen.
She didn't have to do everything her parents wanted her to do!

But she was even more unhappy now
than she had been before she met Dale.
Using heroin didn't solve Lee's low self-
image problem. Heroin only added more

50 | problems to her life. It made her feel worthless.

Lee realized that she had not thought about what might happen when she began using heroin. Now she knew that saying "Yes" to heroin was a bad choice. Lee knew she needed to correct that mistake. She decided to accept her parents' advice and get help.

Lee spent the next year using *methadone* under medical supervision before she finally got well. She spent a lot of time studying and improved her grades. She also joined a school-sponsored "Just Say No" club. There she made drug-free friends.

She found out the hard way that hanging out with junkies would keep her involved with drugs. She wasn't going to make that mistake again!

While Lee was recovering, Dale robbed a service station to steal money for heroin. He ended up in jail. Dale wasn't stupid enough to inject heroin into his veins. But he *was* stupid enough to continue using heroin.

Today, Lee has self-respect for breaking her connection with drugs. She learned to think about the good things in her life. She also learned to concentrate on the

Even bad choices can be turned around. Counselors can help
you change your thinking and your habit.

52 | good things she can do. She feels good about helping herself.

Lee realized that she needed to become her own best friend before she could make other friends.

CHAPTER 3

Summary

In Chapter 2, you read about several teenagers and the choices they made. They didn't all make good choices all the time. There were other good choices they could have made to resist drug use.

We hope their stories give you something to think about when you face peer pressure. A good example of dealing with peer pressure is "Just say No." And looking as if you mean it! There are other ways to avoid trouble. Leave. Ignore the person pressuring you. Joke about it. Set limits ahead of time. Make excuses.

There is no magic way to avoid peer pressure. Find a way that works for you.

The most important thing to remember about drugs is that they are not magic.

Staying away from drinking, smoking, and drugs will help you have a positive self-image.

Drugs cannot solve your problems. You must do that for yourself. And drugs won't help.

Drugs might give you a few minutes of relief. They can make you too confused or too sick to care about anything. But if you're worried, if you don't feel good about yourself, drugs won't cure that.

You need to remember that as a person you have *rights*. Protecting your mind and body is one of your rights. If you stay healthy, does it matter if you aren't "one of the group"?

Former drug users claim that they are most sorry about the damage they did to their mind and body. If you are lucky enough to be drug-free, you have made the most important good choice of your life.

But if you or your friends are involved with tobacco or drugs, it is not too late to correct that with a good choice now.

The list in the back of this book gives the phone numbers of places where you and your friends can get help if you need it.

Think about it.

Then make the choice that is best for you.

Glossary
Explaining New Words

addiction Physical or mental need for a habit-forming substance.

alcoholic Person who cannot stop drinking alcoholic beverages.

AIDS (acquired immune deficiency syndrome) A disease caused by a virus and acquired through sexual contact.

carbon monoxide A colorless, poisonous gas formed when carbon is not completely burned.

central nervous system The brain and spinal cord, which receive messages from the outside world and send messages to the muscles of the body.

crash The physical pain and mental depression that follows the high of a drug.

freebase A paste of cocaine and chemicals that is smoked to give a greater high than cocaine alone.

hooked Being addicted to alcohol or other drugs.

joint A cigarette made of marijuana; also called reefer.

mainline To inject a drug directly into a vein.

methadone A man-made drug that prevents the high of heroin and helps the user stop the use of heroin.

peer pressure Urging by one's friends or social group to undertake a particular action.

snorting Taking a drug by inhaling it.

snuff A form of powdered tobacco that is inhaled, chewed, or placed against the gums.

Help List

Hot Line 800-Cocaine

Answers any questions about caocaine.

- Straight
  24-Hour Prevention Crisis Hotline
  1-800-9-FRIEND

- Al-Anon or Alateen
  P.O. Box 862, Midtown Station
  New York, NY 10018-0862

Look in your telephone book under "Alcohol-ism" to find the telephone numbers of your local chapters of Alateen and Alcoholics Anonymous.

National Association for Children of
Alcoholics
31706 Coast Highway, Suite 201
South Laguna, CA 92677
(714) 499-3889

Students To Offset Peer Pressure
P.O. Box 103, Department S
Hudson, NH 03051-0103

SADD (Students Against Drunk Driving)
Box 800
Marlboro, MA 01752

Telephone Book
Yellow Pages
• Alcoholism, Drug Abuse, Counselors

• Narcotics Anonymous
  World Service Office
  16155 Wyandotte Street
    Van Nuys, CA 91406

For Further Reading

Alexander, Clifton, MD, and Alexander, Sandy. *Kick the Drug Habit.* Tucson: Antler Publishing Corp., 1989.

Browne, David. *Crack and Cocaine.* New York: Gloucester Press, 1987.

Dolmetsche, Paul, and Mauricette, Gail. *Teens Talk about Drugs and Alcoholism.* Garden City, NY: Doubleday & Co., 1987.

Freeman, Jodi, MEd. *How to Drug-Proof Kids.* Albuquerque, NM: The Think Shop, 1989.

Grauer, Neil A. *Drugs and the Law.* New York: Chelsea House,1988.

Hodgkinson, Liz. *Addictions.* New York: Thorsons Publishing Group, 1986.

Hyde, Margaret O. *Mind Drugs.* New York: Dodd, Mead & Co., 1986.

Lee, Essie E. *Breaking the Connection.* New York: Julian Messner, 1988.

Madison, Arnold. *Drugs and You.* New York: Julian Messner, 1982.

Newman, Susan. *You Can Say No to a Drink or a Drug.* New York: The Putnam Group, 1986.

Ryan, Elizabeth A. *Straight Talk about Drugs and Alchohol.* New York: Facts on File, 1989.

Spence, Annette. *Substance Abuse.* New York: Facts on File, 1989.

Ward, Brian R. *Drugs and Drug Abuse.* New York: Franklin Watts, 1987.

Woods, Geraldine and Harold. *Cocaine.* New York: Franklin Watts, 1985.

Index

64 | *About the Authors*

Sue Hurwitz has a M.A. in education and taught every grade K–9. She is the co-author of a young adult biography, *Sally Ride: Shooting For the Stars.*

Nancy Shniderman has a B.S. in computer science and has taught computer camp for teenagers.

Photo Credits
Cover photo: Chuck Peterson
Photos on pages 2, 20, 22–23, 13, 35, 39, 42, 47, 51, 55: Michael F. O'Brien; pages 8, 26: Chris Volpe; pages 17, 19, 29, 32: Stuart Rabinowitz

Design & Production: Blackbirch Graphics, Inc.

14764

362.29   Hurwitz, Sue
Hu

Drugs and your
friends

DATE DUE	BORROWER	
111	Bryon Comocheck	
AUG 29	Destinee Mr Reilly's room	
OCT 01	Gerald Burke / Jeremy Phillips	
89	John Dale 5 A	
JAN 27		

14764

362.29   Hurwitz, Sue
Hu

Drugs and your
friends

Library Media Center
Madison Central School
Madison, N.Y., 13402